returning
to the
light

a collection on *choosing*
healing

olivia morrissey

www.oliviamorrissey.com
@oliviamorrissey__

ISBN-13: 978-1-0933-1832-6

Cover design by Olivia Morrissey

Illustrations by Natalie Woeppel

www.bornofthemoon.com
@natalie_woeppel

For the omnipresent rumbling of all there has ever been.
For the reason of our existence.
For love.

contents

a letter to you

This collection is my winding path from the cave of disillusionment and disconnection to my barehanded claw-climb out of darkness and my flight into the light. This is my journey of reclaiming my love.

We reach the cave the moment we forget that we are love simply because we exist— when we begin to believe, as determined by others, that we are unworthy, undeserving, un-sacred, un-full. And when we choose to consume such limiting, unloving falsities and accept them as truth, we've stepped inside. And when we are inside the cave, we live in a state of fear.

I shed layers of myself— stripped my loud, my bold, my light, my love— in an attempt to become something I hoped would grant me the safe company I had been promised in this twisting lifetime. I changed the shape of my body, my heart, and my spirit in this shadow contract in order to squeeze into a smaller capacity and receive what I thought would be the love I sought. I recreated and redesigned my movements, my thoughts, and my needs to shrink into the space I believed was being asked of me.

I changed the size and capacity of my lungs, the depth of my breath, the network of my capillaries; I lessened the white, the strength, the density of my bones, all in self-proclaimed honorary surrender to the supposed love I shook with bereft aching for.

I knew not yet to recall that the most potent medicine lay waiting, dormant, naturally and eternally within me.

This book is reclamation and healing. It is returning and re-membering. It is choosing the light and choosing to live in your own love. It is the journey back to truth.

May you never find yourself straying too far from you, and may you always remember your way back home if you do.

With love and with light,

Olivia Morrissey

the cave

We chased sweet summertime. A year
and a half of eternal sun. We ran from
darkness, you and I together, without
looking back.

But it caught up to us. And it hit us
smack-dab in the forehead of the
hottest of July days, and it was clear
that nothing light was ever light
without the darkness that makes it so.

The two are beautifully and
frighteningly inseparable. They are one
and always will be.

We were two halves trying to make
whole. Incomplete on our own, so
together we never could be.

— *the awareness*

There was a cool August breeze
blowing
the day I knew I'd lost you

— *chasing eternal summer*

This space
is haunted because of you

A real-life
living color
ghost
that spooks me
with nostalgia of us

Of our haunting
twisted
past
unknown
undiscovered
dark
untrue

We're hurting each other
more and more
by the day

You touch her in my sight
because you know that it tears
for she is a woman
of all of my fears

Giving in to all vices
which you'd leave me to do
and I abstain from mine daily
to safeguard part of my truth

I hit you
with word-venom
and little coiled fists
a broken
broken-hearted child
holding on by frayed string

This space
and you
bring out a hurt
cruel
eerie piece of me

Maybe
after it all
I'm haunted too

Your stings give me no choice
but to fight back
this pain game
must be played
with two

And I don't like
this thing I've become
I know that I'm haunted
too

— *haunted*

Golden flame to golden flame
wavering and ice-hot and all the same
she yearns for the burn of the lesson
she won't learn
in this cyclical ego game

Moth aroused after golden flames
she scars anew but her self is to blame
burning but she is addicted to the game
of golden flames to golden flames

— *golden flames*

Your sweet sandy scent reeks of
needing love

Your calloused hands
need soaking in bubble foam
your jaded ocean eyes
call for a ship to return home

The shape of your head needs love
it calls for kisses and rubs
and I happen to be wearing
ready love-gloves

How my lips were made
to be wooden masts
returning to a lover
after a voyage at sea

And my arms were built
wide and vast
and until its very last
they'll hold your tired heartbeat

And while my sole purpose is
to keep you afloat
the truth of my need

to send you love roots

In much deeper swell
than my crippled heart knows
in that I am the one
who is needing
my own

— *needy love*

This love has punctured new holes in
me
holes where I didn't know holes could
be
and now
I am a sinking ship

I've spent years perfecting makeshift
plugs
of boyfriends
and friendships
and masks
survival tactics

Some holes are obvious
my eyes
and their over-exercised tear ducts
my mouth
as it screams and yearns and begs for
your love
give it to me
please

My arms
and open embrace
one more place

of empty space
the sacred feminine parts of me
that crave your body
inside of mine

Plug me
look me in my eyes and see the ocean
storming behind satin curtains
hold my body close enough to yours
so that nothing else can escape from it
and I don't sink like a stone into the
very waters that are me and possess me

You are a woodpecker
that sits on my oak boat
in the middle of vast seas
it is just you and me here
and for whatever reason
this boat of mine cannot find
one motive
not to cling to your company

Or perhaps I am a tree
planted
rooted
great and strong but slightly wavering

in our love
and you
my woodpecker
from whom I long for a visit
to grace me so
though I know each time
you'll fly away from me

Taking bits
and leaving new holes in me
when you go

— revised from *this love has punctured
new holes in me* originally published on
ThoughtCatalog.com

I miss you in a stadium full of people
loud and crazy and busy
when I'm feeling so very
alone and unknown

I miss you in a bed just us two
quiet and exposed and still
when I'm feeling so very
alone and unknown

— *I miss you*

The sparking start of a love
just a crush
just a hello and
quick word
before you have to go

And it sends chills
and butterflies come
and smiles stay
to replay that minute
all day

But it's never enough
when you want the full-blown
full-force
tangled legs
explored hearts
love

Now
after all this time together
a hello and
quick word
before you have to go

Void of spark

and deepened heart
and one minute with you
is still
the best part of my day
but it's still
never
enough

— *never enough*

I've missed those eyes
he says
we are lying in the grass
under afternoon sun
the light shines truth on everything
we'd rather not
we didn't

How is it that
I never noticed these matching freckles
he asks
mapping me out
by my little cities and towns

Ants are biting me
despite my desire to feel close to the
earth
and to show him how I am
they aim to pinch me back to reality

But I've ignored them
I am in puddle state
and have been
since the moment he touched my inner
thigh

16

My eyes
the ones that after looking at you with
love
looked at you with
fear
resentment
aching
disappointment
hope
lust
pain
and
longing

How could you miss all of that
I didn't host the courage to ask him
and I will never learn his answer
just a taste of love is
that sweet
I suppose

— *when love bites*

To be in your presence at all
even in the worst of conditions
is quite enough
to make me surrender
any other obligation

— *dependence*

I've read poetry
on other lost-lovers' demise
attraction too strong
to fight impulse-arise

Energetic and magnetic
pull to my surprise
your pained hands are lightning
bolts down my thighs

— *lying in the grass with you*

He presses
hard
my buttons
the way he presses
his body to my body
in ways no one has before

He repels
hard
my goodness
the way he turns
his heart from my heart
in ways no one has before

I am stubborn
steadfast
stimulated
by these ways

These body
mind
and heart games

And when I'm in shadow days
I want to play
hard

And I win
hard
until I lose
hard
and fall
hard

— *hard*

Never knew a love could make me feel
so
alone and unloved

— *nighttime thoughts*

Listen to her
when she speaks her words
when her eyes speak them for her
when she tells you
even lightly
gently
that she hurts

That she yearns
craves
needs

For these feelings will build
and the weight then
too heavy
for this single-sided
woven love tunnel
to withstand

— *listen to her*

I don't recognize eyes
that stare back at me
the light has faded

I look instead to find it in your gaze
I shudder
challenged by darker ice

I realize
I am surrounded by black
a sharp foreign place
and I don't have maps

The little girl
who makes fairy homes
in her mother's garden
between lilacs and roses

She doesn't come here
I can't taste her soul
I almost remember
but I pass out in cold

— *this is not who I am*

Fingers
arms and
hands
reaching to grasp
your love

Searching through
the darkness
sifting through covers and
shields and lies

I was never able to find
I was never able
to find
your love

— *I was never able to reach you*

The letter-shapes of your name
make me insane
I get drunk off the thought
of you thinking of me

Words you said in your bed
play on repeat in my head
I get high off the thought
of you needing me

— *don't do drugs*

I see you in dreams but even then I
can't see you
I guess that's symbolic of how much
that I need to

— *blurred vision*

I would pour my love into you
day after day
into your bottomless glistening vase

But I tried
and I emptied
but I see you
and I melt

And I again
would pour into your bottomless vase
for the rest of my hopeless
and tiring days

— *take and give*

Our demons
they danced
in magical prance
in spite-burning trance
engaged with both hands

Intoxicating flight
not one could miss
until it came time
total solar eclipse

The implode
blackness
red-hot when dismissed
the swallowing darkness

The demons
of
our love-abyss

— *our demons*

I fell sick

fell sick

fell sick

for two whole weeks when he finally
left. I lost my voice. I became
incapable of speaking this very trauma-
induced pain of him, this pain of my
own mind. In fact, I had lost [control
of] my mind.

I went to all of the dark places, because
I convinced myself that was where I
needed to go to find him. And my ego
and I would pull us both out of there,
into light, into safety, into love.

—revised from *You Weren't Meant To
Save Each Other* originally published
on ThoughtCatalog.com

You've caused me such pain
that no one's rectifying pleasure
could ever feel the same

— *polarity*

I'm here
she whispers
a sound so faint
and too easy to dismiss

Please
she cries
the word barely
escapes into existence

It hurts
she pulses
stained over
her every expression

And then
finally
exasperated in tone

Come home
she moans
with breathless last hope

She collapses
giving way
caving into her own soul

subsiding
into
my own fragile hold

And I am left no choice
but to sop up her spilled voice
and try to make vows
I've not known how

This pale ghost body
of my broken heart's home
I then drank my own blood
my first step on my own

— *the first conversation (heart + body)*

The root of self-love will carry you
through

— *the faintest whisper*

You can keep my birthday shoes
and my favorite pair of socks
you can keep the frame
fit to hold the landscape
of a dying crisp fall
hanging naked on my wall
you can keep them the way
you kept captive my heart
long after your thirst for it
but too soon yet to part

The reckless negligence
of my things and my needs
in unvisited corners
you left them idly
like some kind of knot
trap-rooting my feet
for as long as I wished
them to come back to me

Barefoot I stand strong
once more just to say
that you may now own them
and all of them again
and as you keep my possessions
my hope is they haunt you
for taking too much of

the un-meantness for you
in dusty dark closets
of your mind-game rooms
hiding all of what
you knew to be true

My heart—
my dragon-skin
worn leather
encompassed heart—
has returned fully to me
and it beats powerfully

And though once punctured and pried
at
in heavy casing it's filled
with thick
sweet
flowing blood

Of the most radiating red
you'll never
taste again

Now the only beating my heart sees
is its own
pulsating with love

of and for my damn reigning self

— *mine (possession)*

I go to the places
I know that you aren't
in my daylight hours
and my starry dark

I outrun you
outplay you
outlive you
you see
until it's your time
to haunt me in dreams

— *the ghost and the escapist I*

You and I have
traded roles haven't we
my once empty-shell mold
love-trying for you
and you ever-trying
to escape me

This ghost of mine
no longer flies
but runs cross country
to evade
your heavy shadow
escaping weighted coats
to bask in ever-sun
and never-shade

Of ghost-white love
and lines of blows
you appear to me
finally
transparent as
you could ever be
chase-haunting me nightly
in inescapable dreams

— *the ghost and the escapist II*

If all I ever knew of you
was 60 percent
and I loved that three-fifths
to its full extent

Does it equal or justify
why you and I
never added up?

My head understands
but my heart keeps
getting stuck

— *the mathematics of love*

I ache for my loving healing
but my mind's convinced
I'm not ready to not need you
for you won't be joining me
on this lightened journey
and I'm not sure you'll be ok on your
own

Or was it that I had myself thinking
broken me
in you
found home

Well either way I know
to my pained and lonesome bones
the faint taste of my truth is calling
and I must leave you alone

— *the faint taste of my truth is calling*

The gentle-men I know don't wear ties
and suits
they wear tees
and they love me
for a night or a few months or just
shy of a year
and they're great at saying promises
and lip pressing sweet nothings to my
ears

They've got the biggest smiles
and the most sparkling eyes
they love a good drink
and they're not like other guys

No
they're like no others
but they are all the same
and they get their greatest thrill
hearing me call their name

But when they're done
and it's time to run
one by one
they go

on bike
on plane
or even on the phone
I've got it down now
and I know

The most courageous of them
will go on foot

No
the gentle-men I know don't wear ties
and suits
and they don't take the time
to pay mind
to their unhealed ties
or to
their unloved roots

So one by one
they always leave
they
and their tees

And they
always

follow
suit

— revised from *the gentle-men I know
don't wear ties and suits* originally
published on ThoughtCatalog.com

I read the aching poetry you write
I see your ocean soul stare with
longing
I can feel the cauldron-depths of your
heart
why do you keep me at a distance?
he says

Because if I let you in
and you like what you see
perhaps you will stay
and I'm not ready for anyone to stay
for I'll be in constant fear of them
leaving

And if you don't like what you see
you will leave
and I will never be ready to be left
again
for you will confirm my deepest fear
that everyone goes eventually

— *heart fear*

You say you're a lifeguard
well I am drowning in this love
EMS certificate
I cannot breathe in this space you've
put me in

Sweet friend
my firefighter
I am in flames
and you are the lighter

Toxic
destructive
unhealthy
this behavior

And you're not here
you're not coming
I know I am my only savior

— *I know I am my only savior (the rescue)* originally published on ThoughtCatalog.com

You claimed my heart
but never created a safe space for me
you never once watered me
your soul-soil was barren
you shined your light at times
and I tried to grow with that alone
but a flower requires much more
to truly blossom
you see

— *a flower requires*

I write and write and write
re-membering you and me
I stretch my ears for spaces I missed
where you might've let me in

I write to twist the frame a bit
to ease some ache
to pain dismiss

And my journals are filled
but my heart's still drained
I decide to shift
this path I've laid

— *the first revision*

the choice

I'm hosting all this loneliness
so to the ocean I go
and in Her waves she whispers
coast to coast *I know*

She holds me in Her massive arms
cradles me close to Her chest-heart
and lullaby-soothes away the pain
until it's time for us to part

It's to my ocean creator I go
with my constant aching heart
for She knows life is death and loss is
love
and all of it is art

She knows the pain of kissing endlessly
sand time after time to only be
pushed back away and pulled devotedly
the way only Her vast heart-space can
be

Full of life and full of love
enough to hold the whole world
in natural fleece and raindrop gloves
and shape us into pearls

Eroding our edges for us to learn

truth
and get naught in return

The ocean is my creator
She is my container
when this world keeps taking away
from me
She holds me fully and lets me be

Her vast embrace swallows me with
love
in natural fleece and raindrop gloves
Her waves whisper always *child I know*
so with my aching heart to her I go

In lullaby sound She sings to me
I love you safely and here you're free
welcome back brave soul to your own
magnificence
traversing physical life with spiritual
limitlessness

Oh it's to the ocean I always flow
coast to coast devotedly so
because it's with Her I am never alone

and only with Her I am always home

— *oceancoming*

Sometimes
when you feel so much love
and empathy
for the population
of the entire world
and it feels like the dam
around your water-heart
has collapsed
and you are absolutely
gushing
surging
and
cascading
outside of yourself

You just need someone
to hold you
tightly enough
to close you up
contain you
take shape as
the barrier around you
that keeps it all in

You
are that encompassing one
for me

Maybe I
am that encompassing one

56

for me

— *beholder*

When he finally left me for the last
time— emotionally, physically,
mentally— he looked me in my eyes
and said, "You are a beautiful person."

And I knew then that I would be the
only one to carry myself into
salvation— into love— and that I was
the only one standing in my own way.

And I knew then that I would be
victorious. I will be my own savior.
And he will be his own savior. And we
will both be beautiful.

— from *You Weren't Meant To Save
Each Other* originally published on
ThoughtCatalog.com

A year in darkness and this is what I've
learned:

That happiness is gratitude
and it's about all you have and not
what you can't see
and that love is the common tongue
trans-culture universally
that it is so much more
about who you're with instead of where
and that peace comes from celebrating
our differences
rather than what is shared

I've learned that true hope is not
never having felt the darkness
it is having been immersed in it
and still choosing to see the light
and strength is not
being devoid of weakness
it is how we accept our weaknesses
and hold them equally tight

I've learned that sometimes
life must hit rock bottom
it must get to the lowest of the low
the darkest of hours
in order for it rise
to lightness once again
the winter solstice

karmic powers

And it is often not what we're dealt
but how we choose to react
that makes all the difference
so let us choose not what's easy
but rather what's right

Let us choose hope
let us choose strength
let us choose ourselves
let us choose love

And let us choose light

— *a new year*

I am whole. I am full. I am enough.

— *the first mantra*

You were not high enough for him
you were too real
too grounded
you were too little
and you were much too much

He could not yet remember
his capacity
to understand
and match and meet
you within himself

And your littleness
your truth's wow
your much-too-muchness
your every sound

This is who you are
your greatest silence loud
in all its just-enoughness
for one single soul to swallow

And one day it will be enough
for someone
somewhere too
but now the soul to know it
accept and love it
is you

— *I was high enough (for me)*

I fell in love with a fantasy
reality—
emotional breadcrumbs—
skewed
distorted and beautified by
my own shiny mind

Paint a little hope on that
a little romance
despair and aching
I want you as deep as possible
if it's not love
that we are making

That mind of mine's got a mind of its
own
how clever it must be
to make me cling
to its own falsity
curating my life
around his un-healing

Well me and my heart
and those two minds
have got enough company
for our own damn time
I guess I never needed you
the way I thought you see
I'll just keep falling in love

with my own fantasies

— *falling in love with fantasies*

If it weren't for you
I wouldn't have broken out of these
chains
never would've
blossomed green growth
and sought through the cracks in your
cement to taste the sunlight

If it weren't for you
I wouldn't have burst toward breath
like out of the spout of a humpback
whale
your air-water-energy pressure
pushing down on me in opposition
has forced me to eruption
to become the exploding supernova that
I am

If it weren't for you
I would've never ruptured through
and I don't plan on being imprisoned
again anytime soon
for all of this I must thank you
oh if it weren't for you

— *if it weren't for you*

I believe in myself.

My faith and self-love are enough to
carry me through.

I love myself.

I am safe now.

I am not alone—
I am with me at all times.

— *reconditioning*

I took my first breath today
it filled my capillaries to entirety
and only mine
just enough and nothing less
and I didn't let it extend to another's
energy
to fill some void of theirs I never could

I didn't offer it away to someone
who wanted it selfishly instead
no matter how seemingly deserving or
less fortunate
I didn't inhale-open my lungs-heart-
arms-soul
for anyone else
just tasted the sweetness for myself

And once I got a taste
I gasped
for more
for air
for another breath of the life lived
when you're living it for your damn
self and yourself alone

And now that I've inhaled
I'll never hold my breath for anyone
else
and I never plan to stop
this circular-motion healing

of sweet breathing to live
and living for breathing

— *breathing for me*

You looked so different face-to-face
with my blurred pragmatism
and heart-swayed vision
from the others
from the previous
than the last
all of the past

But when I catch first glance
in my rearview mirror
after the first inhale
of my at-last breakaway
your face
their faces
the rest
all blend into stale imagery

I don't want anything I've had
I want what I've never tasted
and I will happily
and readily
devour it

— *the taste of now*

These days I only see you in my
dreams
and I get to see you there nightly
I forget what wholeness can almost
mean
until my heart's locked you in
delightfully
in my dream-space I relive solely
the smiling moments on repeat
where all is pure and un-lonely
and I wake from you at ease

Our starry sky is safe from vice
and you've spent all night beside me
no her
just us
no clouds of white
I hold you once more tightly

In truth it is blissful rose-golden deceit
of sweetly-pained selective memory
and dear
it's almost enough for me
but my dear
it was never enough for me

— *this dream is a nightmare*

When I moved across the country
I bought a knife
to cut things for myself

Ropes
fruit
wood

To cut ties
dependency
on other people
on him

A tool for me
and my use

When I moved across the country
I
myself
drank a bottle of expensive red wine
bold Cabernet

A vacant vessel
to dress
my mantelpiece
my mirror-emblem of
the emptiness
the bloody richness
of life
without you—

life for me

— what would Frida do

olivia morrissey

This year
these days
my present is re-writing

Re-wiring
re-adjusting
re-framing
re-claiming

My brain
my heart
my health
my life
my thoughts
my actions
my behaviors
my love
my truth

For I
am my
creator

— *but what do I wish to create*

I am healing without you
scars on my body
binds on my heart
all memories of pain are fading
everything
is lighter
and everything
is continuing to get lighter

— *light*

The lucky ones have been raised
taught
shown the way
by a Queen— a diamond

The rest of them
create more blindly
being from darker spaces
obscured faces
lacking Her royal clarity

And yet
we all must make the choice

For there is no demand
nor guarantee
of an experience of nobility

Of justice
kindness
love
transparency

But the entire cosmos
and all that is of the Universe
is cheering us through
praying this way
is the path that we choose

— *thou mayest choose love*

Oh big old oak tree
give me some stability
remind me what I'm rooted in
that I'm not just passing-by wind

Show me a love to be grounded in
dependable love
who wants to be around and

Hold my body
with the sturdy hands
of a man
who
stands tall and
is strong enough to catch me
whenever I fall
for I'll fall
but I'll be all
right if he's shown up

Grounded
my oak tree
here when I call
to rest upon
and lean on
present fully in all

— *finding grounding*

At the time
you had to grow spikes
and firm walls
to protect
the quenching love-water
that you harnessed
deep inside
because that is what
survival meant
but here you are
after it all
everything is a process
and now
it is time
to bloom

— *it is time to bloom*

the first taste
of the moon

The ocean welcomed me home with
calm
silence and then
sets and currents
and stormy waters

To remind me how
powerful she was
how I was

The sun and air
welcomed me home with
thick humidity

A blanket of warm love
a close hug
until the night made its way
and I went to lie
beneath a canvas of diamond-sky
and the beautiful starry darkness
reminded me why

With a shooting star
crossing cricket sounds
my croaking nature comforted me
and it was home that I found
oh
it was home that I found

— *forever home*

I expected it would happen in stages
I didn't know it would hit so hard in
waves
I know that it's all part of the changing
I am like the moon I too
must go through phases
and I know with you I was complacent
you never sparked my heart
or made me feel I was your favorite
and still I can't seem to replace it
I'm holding on to your coaster love and

I'm not sure that you were the right one
for me
and it doesn't change
I'm not proud to say I do
but I miss you

And I just ignore the low-lows that you
brought into my life
because the highs were so high
and I miss them

It's true the lows are entwined
forever with the highs
it's time for me to own up
selective memory—
it's time for me to grow up
in fact
I recall being high on my own

long before you showed up
Phase two
my moon is new
I'm coming back around
release this coaster love

I know now that you weren't the right
one for me
and it all changed
and I'm proud to say I don't
I don't miss you

I can't just ignore the low-lows you
brought into my life
cause they weren't worth the highs
and I don't need them

— *I am like the moon*

When I am lost, scared, confused,
I can turn to me.

Deep down,
with gentle exploration,
I know that I have all the answers I
need.

Why consult a puddle
when I have oceans inside of me?

I know what's best;
external validation is not what I seek.

— *Monday mantra series*

I found my tongue
and though it's lashed and has run
the past has rung
for me to come undone

I've had my fears
throughout the years
of causing tears
with my truth-tongue mirror

And while it's sharp
it's tied to my heart
and the disconnect that's sparked
voicing fable parts

Is too much to bear
all hearts be spared
for I'm finally there
and I won't not share

My honest truth
down to my roots
this tongue's all but used
to being but a muse

And I won't speak but scream
my mind each time
for it's tied to my soul
and now I'm aligned

Said I've found my tongue
and now I can say
I now speak my truth
for it's the only way

— *I found my tongue II*

I had to become the man
that I needed to be loved by

I had to teach myself the things he
knew
about boats and tents and knives
and learn all that he had learned
about directions and science and skies

So that I could stop seeking a father
out of my teacher-lover companions
and embrace my solitude
as a woman with her man-lens

The loving and learning
the healing and hurting
all had to in time arise

I know I had to become the man
I always needed to be loved by

— *I became the man I needed to be*
loved by

How silly of me
caressing other bodies to feel whole
to think that one could have
sweeter nectar than my own
to yearn for connection deeper
than the temple in which I've grown
years later I'm consoled
intertwined mind body and soul

— *caressing other bodies to feel whole*
(divine intertwine)

3 a.m.
why aren't you my friend
plastic bag in the wind
no— paper it's in
in this land of fruits and nuts
am I really finding myself
or just getting lost?

When the greatest fear of mine
is not seeing that I'm blind
is the seven-chakra shine
really altering my life-design?
I cannot seem to define
what is theirs and what is mine
or draw a line of love from
driving fear hiding inside

Am I learning secrets greater than man
or cult-ing to be burned at the witches'
stand?
is my healing path not what is for me
that which doesn't steal from my
capability?
am I less bright or change-making if I
choose to be
naked praising moonlight and healing
poetically?
with dreams to connect us all
with heartfelt possibility
have I lost the end-goal

and fallen for conspiracy?

When my deepest life-addiction
is in yearning for my conviction
and my return to earth from
codependency
is the healthiest form that I can see
in loving something kind and true
and receiving loving back to me
do I listen to voices that fear
and question my recent well-being?

When the mountains protect me
and the ocean sings me to sleep
and the moon dictates my life cycle
is this really all a cheat
has a cult life taken over me?
or am I learning to trust the Universe
to heart-read and write and speak
all the love I've forgotten I was
of which all the cosmos is reminding
me

— *spiritual spiral*

Keep snorting your white
I choose gently inhaling
sweet breath late at night

Go on
let the alcohol
swim through your veins
I will let love run through mine
and release my disdain

You can swallow your crystals
and also your pills
I will full-moon charge mine
and swallow my pride

I'll catch secondhand good vibes
and firsthand gratitude
you rearrange the serotonin in your
brain
I adjust my attitude

Consume-wish-rely on your drugs
to bring you to a higher state
as for me
I choose to meditate

— *drug of choice (getting high)*

I had a dream I saw you as a child
and I looked deeply into your eyes
caught your glance from afar and held
it
for far too long

Maybe I could catch you
before it all started
before the hurt made you hard

Maybe I could see into those glassy
seas
that were vast and distant and beautiful
but cut like knives all the same

What's going on in those oceans inside
you
maybe I could just see
and exchange love for love

Earlier
sooner
than when it was our tough time and
trial

Maybe I could understand
what's more
maybe you could finally see me

— *glassy seas*

I just got lost
he says
and it breaks my heart to hear
because I lost sight of us
in the meantime

And all I can do
and all I could've done
is be someone
who shines light on your love
and all the ways and pieces
of you that are love
and hope you use that flashlight
to find your own way home

For I could only ever be your vessel
and space
once the welcome mat to welcome you
first is your own

— *come home*

I feel more than ever in this new state of living that a veil has been lifted. I am so much more honest with myself, which allows me to be honest and direct with others, and it makes my relationships more clear, true, and fulfilling. I'm showering myself first in self-love and positive, healthy mantras, and I am attracting people who see that and want to treat me the same— with love.

It's as if a veil, a film, a screen has been lifted— it is all about perspective. Two people can be dealt the same experiences and handle and view them so differently. I was living so blindly before, not knowing I had the power to change everything. It is the world's greatest secret. I feel at peace, and I am only ever-learning.

— *full moon, full of peace, full of life* a journal entry

To all of the men
who have ever said
of a woman
that she was bad in bed:

She is not bad at sex
no one is bad at sex
she does not lack the desire to jump
bones
nor the willingness
you simply
did not tap into the Source
of her divine Goddess-ness

Inside of Her eternity
there is a well
holy and glistening and endless

Still water until found
fierce tiger low and crouched
and born ready to pounce

Into a waterfall
oh— to drown in a waterfall

Silly man how can your mouth
jump to making so much noise
slewing *you've had better*
standing scarecrow tall

When you created no safe space
or sacred poise
for her mouth
her body
to wish to open at all?

— *open mouths*

I kiss the flower head
beside my bed
and I blow out the candle flame
then
I make my own legs shake
whisper *I love you*
and roll over to sleep
cradling my own curves and dreams

— *nights without you (nights with me)*

I am capable.

I am deserving.

I am whole.

I am full.

I am enough.

I believe in myself.

I am trying my best.

It's all a process.

It's OK. Everything is OK.

I am my actions and energy.

I AM THE TIGER.

I live life with my heart.

I live a life of abundance.

I receive life's love and abundance.

I trust healing.

It is safe to heal.

— one year of mirror mantras

I used to think I wanted someone
without baggage. Someone who's
never had to hurt or cry or be pained or
was left or lost or cheated on. Someone
who was healthy. Someone who knew
what healing was.

But healthy is not never having been
hurt. By order of non-duality, and only
in contrast, healthiness and healing
exist with unhealthiness, toxicity, hurt.

One is not healed if they've never been
hurt. Perhaps they are content— I'm
sure they are content. And there are
times I wish I could have journeyed
with such contentment.

But everyone has been hurt. And I'll
take that hurt and pain because it gives
way to my healing.

I am not strong because I have never
been weak. I am strong because life has
brought me to my knees and yet I
choose to stand.

I am neither happy nor joyous nor
smiling because I have not experienced
despair. I am smiling joyously because

my despair has allowed me to feel
extreme bliss in comparison.

I have baggage. Baggage that has
weighed me down so close to the cold
earth that even the dream of flying felt
like a distant wish.

Yet I am checking this baggage, piece
by piece, and it allows me the
opportunity to let go, to release, to heal.

It has given me the precise skill sets
and understanding and experience-
opportunity to self-heal, to self-love.

We all have baggage. And I have
decided I am not the attendant to ask
myself, nor another, not to.

It is all about how— how, on our
journey, are we taking care of and
managing and loving our baggage?

And I choose love-checking mine. And
I now dream that my honey love-
checks their own baggage, too.

And then,
only then,

do we take flight.

— *bag lady* a journal entry

Oh body
I want to make a home in you
I want to adorn you with decor of
kindness
serenity and belief

I wish to fill you with natural light
the light of compassion
I seek to sign harmonious contracts
with my tenant emotions

I crave to dance liberated within you
to the sound of my own joyous laughter
to the electric guitar that is my heart

I hunger to create delicious home-
cooked magic within you
mouthwatering thought-alchemy that
nourishes my future
my present

I desire to make love inside you
to keep it stirring on the stovetop ready
to expand
rising to heat so pulsating
so white hot
as to burst through the walls of all of
my senses
so that the neighbors hear

I aim to grow in you
and then retreat within you
when I ache for a break from the rest of
the world
recluse to your multiverse
back to my own favorite company
feeling safe-sound and secure

I choose to paint you with intention
with the finest oils and creams
I commit to hanging dreamcatchers in
my mind
to welcome bliss home while I sleep

I vow to warm you with the fire of
sacred wisdom
and embodiment of the divine
I pledge to lock you from unwanted
visitors
and keep your doors
wide open with a summer's breeze
to all whom in love arrive

Oh body
I've so long wanted to be home in you
I've bid a lifetime lease

Oh body
I am at last home within you
I am finally

at peace

— *finding home* originally published
on YogiApproved.com

I am owning
my
self.

My
life.

My
sexuality.

My
opinions.

ME

And I feel free.

— *embodying*

I have chanted
I have lain nude under the full moon
I have burned herbs
inhaled shamanistic medicine too
I've recharged my main chakras
release-cried from meditations
and swapped crystals in for crosses
tracked my bleeding to lunar phases
I've held many hands
and embraced many strangers
I manifest with magical statements
and have seen unfolding dreams take
place
so would I sink or would I swim
with nature's rocks to weigh me down
call me a witch to burn at stake
for I am flying and will not drown

— *I am flying and will not drown*

This Scorpio tongue speaks
the truth I ever seek

I am the woman that I love
I'm the light
and the wisdom there ever was

I am her confidence and poise
I am her silence and her noise
I am her seduction
I am her divine
I am her love
and her love is mine

I am the one I've always sought
I am the answer I've so long fought
it is me and I am here
I firmly decline a life in past fears

I am the water
I am a queen
I am my present
I am my dream
I am the earth
I am the moon
I take up space
and claim my room

I voice my needs and I speak my mind
this journey of healing has taken some

time
but I now listen deeply to sing my song
for it's been me
it's been me all along

— *Scorpio full moon meditation*

Don't you ever get complacent with me
true concern comes with closed teeth
one swallows silence
to starve by meals that don't feed
I will always spit back
fear that rises up in me
out-moaning the noises
masked as needy sensitivity

True concern comes with closed teeth
I thirst for shared exhales we breathe
mouth to neck and fuming
processing we need
survival is addressing
all that seeks to be seen
silence is far too loud
complacency is giving up on me

— *new needs, new me*

I follow his eyes
way down to my thighs
I wait for their rise
and I catch his surprise

It's not his demise   .
though I'll watch as he tries
to make love to my ties
stress-holding thigh-cries
from the pain that's inside

But I'll teach with eyes wise
he who strokes in love-strides
to hold space of this size
so that one day we'll lie
and he'll drink my reprieve

I let him enter
this thick
heart-temple of mine

— *emotional body*

Apologies for my timidity
my mixed signals and all that
poor boy you should know
you must treat me like a cat

Touch me just temptingly
play hard-to-get gently
never shift
or speak
too soon

I'm observant as ever
and I see your every move
don't you scare me
and ruin
the mood

I am a recovering addict
not booze nor drugs no
but of pain and heartache
and hurt men so

Be careful hey
with all your good
I'm just not ready
the way I should

Don't push too fast
with all your light
and tender-soft lips

and treat-you-right

But there is a heart there
I promise I'm just scared
and if you're patient and slow
and maybe just do not stare
so much
or reveal
that you're falling
in love

I think I just may
fall for you too
and when I fall
I fall in sticky glue
I will forever be loving
and devoted to you

So be sure this is what you want
passion comes at a slow start
but once it gets going
I host a full ocean
rivers
lakes
and streams all in motion

And they're always
flowing
and they're never
slowing

and I will keep on
rowing
tending to love
ever-growing

— *cats don't like water*

Sometimes I believe it fair
to wish them fair warning
I am no fair-weather woman
to be left come morning

I am also not a woman
shallow enough to dip toes in
for you to mosey in
stick your nose in
and deem my love too hot
and my independence too frozen

Sometimes I believe it fair
to wish them fair warning
I am a tidal wave
expansive-vast enough to drown
I am the great ocean
I make love in sea-sound

I don't host much expectation
and no longer hope
for curious sailors
with plans to float

My sets of feeling
and waves of healing
desire no fair-weather
seafarer to pry near me

But one who knows

my heart he might die in
and one who still
chooses to dive in

— *I am no fair-weather woman*

olivia morrissey

Her stormy waters
entice me most
for they remind me
I'm not alone
in wrath and in shadow
my dark and my depth
my healing and cycles
my secrets best kept

— *her darkness makes her light*

I will paint the picture
she stares
pursed dust-rose lips
pale face flushed with winter's kiss
wide sea eyes
deep in trance
at the cream coral sun
whispering over the Atlantic
songs of a French café
unfold in a mental soundtrack

She is aching
achingly beautiful
and she is here right now
heads turn to catch a moment
of her mysterious giving presence

She is learning to be selfish
but she is un-near the present
for her mind is afar
romantically attuned
to thoughts of you
in thoughts of blue

Fantasized wishes
of what may never come true
in thoughts of whom
she wishes she knew

— once a romantic, always a romantic

These days
to ocean soundtrack and lines of waves
I exhale you
with stifled lungs
I've passed by
the good that encircles me near
to ensure I always reserve vacant space
for your aversion to ever be here

These nights
to white and purple crystal lights
I exhale you
burning candles as a ceremony
releasing you is like a pheromone
I can finally invite in through open
teeth
to quench a dying thirst of many moons
I make room from you
and I make room for me

These mornings
in hills and valleys into which I'm
lowering
I exhale you
step by step of my hiking boots
it's happened in tiny bits you see
I let you go here
and look up to him smiling at me

I suppose I'll be okay

without this old memory
and he and I chase each other
through whispering trees
train stations and mountain ranges and
this bit here of you
I know now that it must go too
I am safe in letting
my expansion slip past you

In opening up this unloving space
I inhale me and good awaits
I am free to aerate full-bodily
completely
and it's all new breath
that I am breathing
I am here to finally
breathe anew
I am inhaling me deeply
for I am exhaling you

— *breathing freely (exhaling you)*

When you're present
the trees will wave at you
the flowers will release sweet perfume
for your inhale
the waves will somersault
for your pleasure
the mountains will breathe
but only
when you
are present

— *dance for the flowers*

Wow
she is really discovering
how powerful she is
huh

Yes
yes
I am

— *crystal clear*

I am earth
ground and
sound and
I am flowers
like the one you gave me
I am trees
you are water
cool and
wet and
washing over me
quenching
cleansed
I can breathe
you revive me

And together
earth and water
ocean softening mountain
soil rooting fountains
there is life
and with life
there is love

— *earth and water*

My softly tangled
vined heart
my deeply rooted
tree-trunk body
my soul of grass and ground
seeds and soil
ache for rain
like the very earth itself
together we play
refill and dance
connecting beneath wet droplets
together
we rejoice

— *learning to drink*

I am a woman of many facets
rock faces and desires
and what I would like for you to do
is know them over time
but there are no hardened edges here
and they're all really quite smooth
I suppose that makes me curvy
and much fuller hands for you

— *I am a handful*

Grip me not by the stem but
caress my petals and
kiss dew drops from my folds
it is here in this way that I will open
any other way will find me closed

— *sapiosexual*

I am fire
reckless
desert
heat
I am fiery
passion
destruction
at least
in daydreams
you see
sometimes
I grow tired
of being subtle earth
sometimes
I crave
elemental redesign
just one time
I want to be
liberated fire
and not grounded
earthy desire
but then I remember
I am trees
quiet growth
subtle soil of seeds
wildflower fields
and gardens and weeds
and fire
might
just

kill
me

— out of my element

Fierce feminine
empowered with humility
twisting with pleasure
knowing
wild

Awakening within
to share without

me
me
me

Authentic
fully embodied
me

— *swallowing the moon*

the return

I tried something new today in my
nude mirror gazing practice... I adorned
myself with my favorite pieces of gold
jewelry.

It was such a sight to see, my natural,
physical body adorned like that,
making me feel like the sacred, divine
woman I am.

I felt like the magic royalty I am simply
because I am a divine creation of the
Universe, of Source, of God; I felt the
beauty and royalty that I have been
reclaiming in the past year or so.

A huge lesson for me in this lifetime is
in the giving away of my own power.
My intuition, worth, sex— that I have
so often done.

I have put a lot of energy towards
reclaiming this in all aspects of my life
in the past year or so, and some days it
feels like justice. Some days it feels
like over-compensation. And every
day, it feels like I am learning to love
myself and forgive myself more.

But today, I feel like the queen I am.

— *one month of mirror gazing*

There are times when I catch myself
imagining
how beautiful I'll be able to see myself
at the end of this physical life
when I can see with clarity
the wholeness
the enchantment
the depth
that I really am
that I always was
but was too blind to witness
in every day of this earthly existence

Then
there are times when I catch myself
imagining
how beautiful it would be
to allow me to see myself
in my present reflection

No
I do not want to wait
yes
I do not have to wait
now
when I look in the mirror
I stare courageously into my own ocean
eyes
and say

Little girl
grown woman
you are magic
you are a sacred queen
and yes

For the sake of all of the thunder
the lightning
the gardens
the tornados
and the mountains
that exist to reflect your natural wonder

You
are
beautiful

— *grown woman, you are magic*

I saw him tonight

I still
after all of this time
want to take him home
and jump his bones
and be jumped by him
and receive like the desert so aching for
the rain
one droplet of his love

I still
hug him as if he were my own
as if his existence depended on it
as if my own depended on his
I realize this is unhealthy— un-healing

But I come home
and I go to the same bars
and I see you there
and every sweater I see I believe
is from South America
I believe could be encompassing you

Yes
there are pieces
there are shadows
so deep
so large
so dark

that ache
still
for the small capacity
of your love
for me

— *I am triggered*

Do not look to your left
nor to your right
when you are doing this work
it is yours alone

Not one soul began
in precisely your coordinates
and with what you had
and what you didn't have

And not one being's alchemy
is indistinguishable from your own
your holy transmutation
of pain into love
your mold-transfiguration
to great lion from scared cub

Of ache from the heart
of broken back to start

Do not look to your left
nor to your right

Your work is yours alone
commendable
worthy
all on its own

And to swivel your nose
hand-delivers in gold

the medicinal healing
your garden needs to grow

— *your eyes on you*

olivia morrissey

Do you not trust you will one day be
with your Beloved?

Then let this one go

— *the message*

I write of all of my lovers in lifetimes
long lost
ancient heart-harp songs
string into present dreams
reminders of what has been
and what might just be again

It is you— over and over
in all lifetimes through

In this current shape and vessel
in this human role right now
my patience wavers to re-find you
I just can't remember how

How do you look
this time around
what do you feel like how
do you taste inside my mouth
how do you move
where are you bound
do I feel lost
do you feel found

I'll know you by your scent
you will always smell like home
earth and wood and nature
I love you each time to my bones

— *lifetimes love*

Meet me lying in wet grass
early Sunday morning
meet me in the corner booth of a dark
bar
martini kisses on lips
on necks
meet me in the ocean
halfway between steadfast standing
and renounced control to waves

Surrender
meet me by light
candlelight
moonlight
sunset light

And then
follow me
curiously
enduringly
into darkness
and meet me back
lying in wet grass
early Sunday morning

— but first, meet me

In my safest moments, I remember
what it feels like to be soft.

I remember what it feels like to be
unburned: to be warm, to be
illuminated, to be carefree, uncontained
liquid love.

I remember it feeling like magic.

— from *A Letter to the Hardened
Pieces of My Heart* originally
published on elephantjournal.com

Dear Hardened Pieces of My Heart,

Perhaps you don't need to keep a guard up. Perhaps that only perpetuates the connection culture where people play mind games in fear of being hurt and end up hurting others.

Maybe I can love the hell out of myself so hard that I show up for people only out of blazing love, too. Maybe, just maybe, that is something that I myself can do.

Love,

Me

— from *A Letter to the Hardened Pieces of My Heart* originally published on elephantjournal.com

My paintbrush
does shy justice
to the earthly (and also)
divine
taste of you
that I have just barely consumed

I can much better
(though inevitably
falling short)
paint the sweet inhalation
of promising
tantalizing
pheromones that are you
with colorful verbs

I know the droplets of you
that have merely touched
my tongue
are like the words
that sit
on its very tip
ones that I may never find
in our limiting
language to describe
your deliciousness

And what's worse
the intoxication
of the memory

of my first taste
of you

— *tumbling (making purple)*

I'm so attracted to you
for being attracted to me
in this new chapter of my life
where I'm so in love with
and attracted to myself
it is beyond sexy
it is loving
of you
to see this goodness
radiating out of me
and to match it with your own

It makes me want to
soak in this
sweet
buzzing
present
and just listen
as you talk
and just look
and watch
and maybe
just maybe
we can kiss

— *a better buzz (law of attraction)*

Should you find patient
calming
persistent ways
to love me

When I burn like fire
when I strike like lightning
when I destroy
like a reckless tornado
when I am stuck
in my own black-hole depths
and my oceans
swallow and drown

I will find
devoted
wholesome
passionate ways
to love you

When I am music and laughter
when I am gentle green waves
when I touch and feel like velvet
and I am gardens in bloom

When I kiss skin
like warm summer breeze
when I am long-awaited rain
when I see you with cosmos-eyes
and when I am sun

stars
and moon

— *my love*

Sharing space with your soul
is full of bits of gemstone
as much as it is something
I feel I've always known

I believe our colors knew each other
many moons ago
and now we've just met back in sand
in this oceanic home

— *treasure returned*

He breathes new breath into me
weaves turned leaves into trees
deep within my soul seas

Warms heart-honey
running the length of my veins
smiling with the Universe
with me
he plays

Making love to sunrise
and night sky with wide eyes
he plants joy unafraid
bit by bit in his days
he creates

And he knows not
how the light of his eyes
make even the brightest stars in the sky
double take

He breathes new breath into me
full moonlight wishes also to persuade
all great magic to align with love in his
way

His lightest exhale reaches my bone
and I look beside my own humble
throne
where he sits also on love and on gold

and I
am blown
away

— *he breathes new breath into me*

With jasmine-petal breath
and the gentle warmth of sunrise
breaching horizon's crest
after spiraled dark of nighttime

Have you ever been kissed
all the way back down to softness
right here where you exist
where your freely-open heart is?

— *I want to kiss you*

olivia morrissey

I take steps away from fear
and toward love
away from confusion
and toward trust
away from indecision
and toward action
away from misdirection
and toward my path again

— *walking into the waves*

Do you remember
do you remember
that which you loved before you had to
claim it
to name it
to commodify it and explain it

Do you remember
what it feels like to be soft
to be cracked open
and overflowing
to be the river and not the rock

Do you remember
what ignited a spark
deep underneath the protective wraps
of your heart
that which made your spirit start

You remember
you remember
all too loudly when you're quiet

So let's get quiet
let's all get quiet
return to each other
and unite in riot

Choosing our joy
our love

our light
the very truths
we can no longer deny

You are gifted
you are strong
supported and lifted
you are not wrong

You are safe
you are capable
you are great
you are able

You are love
simply
because
you exist
it is time for the unlearning
it is no longer time to resist

Do you feel it
are you listening

It's time to honor your light
and claim your shadow
renounce your fight
surrender your ego

Listen to the faint spark

deep within your center-heart
because you are raw magic
in all of your parts

Do you remember
do you remember
do you remember how
the time is indeed now
it is time to start

— *you remember*

Howling. My truth is howling.

— *dreaming of wolves*

Lights are flashing
I am swallowed in a sea of people
yet I feel
the faintest drop
of a folded note
fall from my pocket

I don't have to pick it up
to know what it says
the words
memories
fear
and aching
I've carried from pant pocket to pocket
and in my head

It reads
of our love
our pain
my delusion
your disdain
repeat

Lies
loss of self
of me
of you
addiction
codependency
truth untrue

Intuition silent
heart gone quiet
I am lost
you drown in black

I would surrender
what is left of me
if only to go back

To the girl who knew
that you can't fix another's hurt
eye to eye saying *child*
yours is the only work

I know
etched
in the pathways of my brain
the river-trees
that are my veins
every word
memory
fear
and ache
on that faded paper
heavy and stained

Lights are flashing
I am swallowed in a sea of people
and still I feel
the faintest drop

of a folded note
fall from my pocket
fall far away from me

And for the first time
in a long time
I don't have to pick it back up at all
and for the first time
in a long time
I don't have to carry you with me

— *paperweight (I now choose to do my
own work)*

Here is the room on your left
(you were not right)
I'll close the door and lock it behind
you

In there you'll find a handful of others
none like you
all like you
blonde and blue
blonde and blue

If you're still lost on what to say
(with your words
you never really did follow through)
there will be a jar of scripts
take one
I already gave you a take-two

I'm sorry
I was wrong
I just didn't know
any better
should've never
let you go
I'm trying
you should trust me
I'm crying
it's not a show

You're my only
though I cheated
it's not drugs
that I needed
I know I left you
I don't expect you
to put it all behind
though I know that you will
because you're pure
and you're kind

And in there you'll find a handful of
others
none for you
all for you
blonde and blue
blonde and blue

There is the room on your left
(you were not right all of you)
the manipulative and smart
the sweet and the tart
the hurt in your heart

I'll close the door and lock it behind
you
other doors are opening
and I'm walking through
this fun house is no longer fun for me
too

164

olivia morrissey

but you all enjoy it in there
my old blondes and my blues

— *room full of mirrors (blondes and
blues)*

I remember the first time
we all got into the same 21+ bar
like it was
some kind of secret club
I remember years of
swimming naked after
sweaty dancing
I remember my first love
I remember the one that came after
and I remember
coming home
year after year
summer after summer
bar after bar
to lie in the grass
of my parents' front yard
beneath moons full
in-love charged
and now
I come here
having passed years
and the moon meets me
just the same
but everything else
oh everything about
this old place
has changed

— *growing pains*

Suddenly—
a layer of sparkling
white
light reflecting
bone-chilling
snowfall
offers new clarity
I have been sitting pretty
squatting
with delusional everlasting guard
upon my pile of suffering

Three hundred and sixty-five days later
a single pivotal change
I don't want to sit here any longer
and with eyes clear
mind still
heart open
I understand unveiled
I have a choice

I don't see aggressors
I don't see cheaters
I don't see liars
I don't see takers
I see humans

Humans who have been hurt
humans who have hurt
humans who are flawed

humans who make mistakes
humans who have a choice

I see me
for the flawed
hurt
trying
human that I am
that I have been
and I decide
it is enough
and I decide
I am ready
and I choose
forgiveness
of myself
of my parents
of my lovers
of all the others

And this
has made
all the difference

And suddenly—
I
have found
healing

— *I don't want to sit here any longer*

I am learning to value my gifts to the
world

purity
warmth
goodness
vulnerability
expression
connection

my love

— *a truer reflection*

I remember the girl that I was
the girl who loved him
who didn't know she loved herself

Though she never knew me
I know her well
and while I can no longer be her
I love her still

For what she knew
for what she didn't know
for the uprooting she would do
for all she weeded and sowed

The persistent nourishing
the love and the watering

That girl
who loved him
who didn't know she loved herself

She is my spinebone
my soul's
favorite gardener

And when I look into crystalline
eyes that are mine
I bow to her Honor
scraped-knee traumas

Of blood and in dirt
and I hold her cut hands
and I hold her heart's hurt
and I turn

To face
the sun

And together
we surrender

And we witness
ourselves

We finally allow
ourselves

To bloom

— revised from *my favorite gardener*
originally published on
elephantjournal.com

Can you see
there are times I will need you to be the
ocean
to cradle me
guide me
cleanse me

There are times I will need you to be
the mountain
to raise me
challenge me
push me

There are times I will need you to be
the earth
to support me
nourish me
root me

There are times I will need you to be
the air
to excite me
move me
breathe me

And times still when I will need you
to be the fire
to ignite me
to resurrect me
to fuel me

And then there are times
most of the time
when I will need to be all of these
things for me
so that I can be all of these things for
you

And that
is why
I spend so much time in nature

— *I'm getting ready for you*

Three weeks numbered our separation
my reservation
for life much less in beauty

Yet when I returned
flushed pink how she yearned
the sunset hugged me

Enveloped me in wispy rounds of
peach
encompassing–holding me
with all of her reach

Sliding with fingers
through covers and walls
with arms of divinity
through forests and halls
to gather me sound
compressed all around
chest fully to crown

The sunset
welcomed
me home

— *sunsetcoming*

Breaths in ride on falls of water and
carpets of stardust
that travel through my body to
flowered Her
and a woman appears
giggling from love and joyful play
you are wet
you taste like delicious earth
you are beautiful
look
see
you try
She says
and She is gone

And He appears
eyes wise
eyes wide
glory eyes
but only for the
moment's reminder that I am the
teacher
the learned
the powerful
the all-knowing
of me

Breaths out ride on pressed temples
and I remember that
I am the keeper of my waterfall and

lava and cosmos
and only I may open the chambers of
their activation
I am the thunderstorm
the rain
the stars and Universe and
the great night sky

And they are both gone
but my feminine creatrix-ness and I
are here
and we
are never leaving

— *journey inward*

I want to inhale
I want to
arms wide open

It entails
steady breathing
slow motion
open receiving
small doses
it grows
it grows

Reception
transmission
the receiving
and believing
I want to feel it
in my bones
I want to
I want to know

I open my heart
it's not so far
when I'm
listening
when I'm
receiving
the guidance that
I'm needing

Because my
head is open
and facing
the ocean
the Universe
is listening
it's set in motion

All that I have
in my heart's desire
this fire
within my womb
my full moon
in the shedding
of what I'm
no longer needing
my body is reclaiming
nutrition and new meaning

And I let go of
this seed and
return it
to Mama Gaia
and she takes
me higher
I know this
deep desire
connecting
to my Mother
respecting

of my Father
ancestors
to discover
the secrets
within another

Oh
I surrender
oh I do
I surrender
my Universe
I surrender
my Higher Source
I surrender to you

— *surrender song (sacred bleeding)*

I've co-created new life joy
reconstructed habits and
repaved my story
to bask in my love where I
used to feel void and

Still
with the slip of wet skin on skin
between the fractures of my healing
chest
through the delicate folds of my space
of dreams
you find me
you have never left me

And when I wake in the morning from
you
there is weight I cannot shake
you remain near me in rearview
as I process our time again

Twisted memories of the shell of me
collapsing into potholes beneath
the hurt that was dealt to you
the hurt that I dealt to me

The dark
and dim cement path
broken glass-laden and
loud with emptiness

Where one soul has chosen failingly
sacrilegiously
inevitably
sacrificially
itself for another
who makes no choice
to choose themself on this
wintry trail without cover
this cold pitch black and
lackluster
street
the road of un-love
was too much a feat

Still
there are times when I wake from you
and you remain with me all day
heavy on my chest and fused onto my
brain
and I know your presence is here to
stay
just so that I must learn to replay
each memory again in streetlamp ways

Infusing my own love into the cracks
lighting the turns and all the
switchbacks
into the old winding lanes
of the old broken days
that you and I once made

that you and I once paved

— *forever repaving*

I woke myself up from enlightened
dreamland
coming to consciousness stretching
in child's pose
4:36 a.m.

Too liberated from what I had just
experienced
I lay awake in bodily expansion
arms— legs
outstretched to claim the space I had
just witnessed

I was there
in dream-space
dancing freely
with an air
and confidence
of authenticity
wholeness

Movements of innate wisdom
twists of plant medicine
a lover
womanly
a truth keeper
holistically
bows of tantric wellness
a healer
a swayer

of life

I stretched in this dream
yoga
I was inside of my body
I was outside of my head
a knowledgeable source
of earthly healing

Having received teachings
having serviced teachings
a guide
a heart nurturer
a space holder
of women's ruling of themselves
of femininity reclaimed

An empowerer
empowered
an empress
of her empire
I danced
with the air of a queen who knew her
worth like
the freedom of her ecstatic movements
depended on it
for they did

Grace
surrender

flow
I was there

And now that I've awakened
to the only dream sweeter than
fantasy—
reality

I renounce my doubts
I release my hows
I inhale my now
into the great Universe divine
the joyous unfolding that is time
I am coming for mine
I am here

— *the dream*

And I forgive him.

And it took every single day. And it
still takes every single day.

And when we re-met, it was the same
old everything— it was the space that I
don't live in anymore.

It was the space of living in fear and
playing it small and holding onto pain.

And I forgive me.

I forgive me for needing that energy,
because I discovered that I am ok
without it.

I am fueled by love, connection,
worthiness, support, excitement on my
own— even more so.

I wish goodness upon him. I fall to my
knees with our fulfilled contracts to
each other. With our experience. Thank
you.

I wish goodness upon us all— for I
wish every single soul to feel the magic
I have just begun to feel about myself

and my life. This choosing me. This
choosing love. This choosing light.

— *forgiveness is freedom*

I am ever-spiraling back to me
in the mirrors I see
and the lovers I seek
in the food that I eat
it is not just me
but Mama Planet I greet

I am ever-twisting
down all paths that lead
myself back to me
and earth green beneath feet

And when I lift eyes to reach
my One locked-gaze deep
I'll know that every soul
every trauma that I meet
each connection that I reap
each lesson that I teach
was just the old way
back home to his sweet
and my ever-return
back to the seed
back to the heart
back to the truth
back to the earth

The return
back to me

— *it is all about the return*

the light

Hello
sweet songbird
you came to me
singing the soul of my truth-speak
and I wrapped naked in bed sheets
outside listening to sunrise-bird tweets
have been waiting for you
I have been waiting for you
oh for so much longer
than I ever even knew

*— mornings with me (mornings
without you)*

I open up my left palm
face up for receiving
surrounded in Ojai by
bumblebees being

And I hear in my well
of divine feminine breathing
it's too much I can't
I don't deserve it really

And at the rise of these words
I find myself shocked
in my stomach pit my back heart
up to my throat block

But my cells remind me
with every moment's breath
that I am God's daughter
made of star-source elements

And I with each inhale
in my body deserve it
and it's never too much
and I'm not limited by *can't*

And I expand my palm size and

let more oxygen glide in
and I open my mouth wide
drink my first big gulps in Ojai

I allow the inner water
to flow now once again
and it's in these endless depths
I remember how to swim

— *divine feminine flow*

I've been living in resistance
oh the world that I exist in
has been so hard
and heavy

And I know I have a choice
to lead from love and then rejoice
instead of the weighted fear
I'm carrying

Oh I aim to be
oh I am to be
like water

And the softness that we are
and the guidance that comes
from living with your
heart-drum

Oh to meet you at my best
eye to eye and chest to chest
free flowing dance of
giving and
receiving

Oh to be like water

olivia morrissey

I seek to be like water
only to be like water

So wash me clean

I want to see you without a lens of fear
I want to breathe you in full
and hear you clear
I want to hold you bone deep
and feel you near
to me

And it's my time to open wide
I know my hopes deserve a try
I big-mouth gulp this now
we call life

And with love-water in my veins
I let the ocean permeate
the dense walls of my fears melt
away

I live to be like water
I love to be like water
meet me here dear
in water

For here we're free
for here we're free

— *like water* a song

Remember that fairies are real
they need garden homes built
flower beds

That trees whisper and tell you where
to go
when to go
that treats are yummy
but so is playing in the sunshine

Cuddling is your favorite— it's how
you feel safe and loved
that is why you crave physical touch
you can trust others to hold you too
every once in a while

Play more
everything will get done

Stay true to you
remember me

Laugh and smile with me
ask me
care for me
dance and play with me

nourish me
encourage me to go outside
speak all of my feelings
imagine with me
listen to me
love me

Know that I am safe now
and everything is ok
I will always forgive you
and I have always been safe with you

— *letter from my six-year-old self*

Stay soft.

When I wake up in the morning
rainfall rolling
down leaves like beads
mouth wide open
I drink and receive

The flow of my Mother
Brother river
Father sea
Sister forest
and plants within
Her and inside of me

I speak for the trees
bow down to Mama Earth
I speak for the trees
root like dirt holds seeds
I speak for the trees
let rainfall wash all over me
pray to the Celestine

I am here
I see
to speak
for the trees

— *unearthing my purpose*

I am here to hold-protect-nurture you
until you remember you are
safe with yourself
then I will love you from afar
until you remember it feels
nourishing
to at times feel close
then I will love you entwined
until you remember we are
always one
then I will love you
as you love me
and I will love me
as I love you

— *divine masculine to my divine
feminine*

When the divine masculine within is
the one to hold protective, sacred space
for my own feminine to dance freely,
that is equilibrium. That is liberation.
That is my love, my truth, my
wholeness.

— *energetic balance*

It is time to let go
it is time to be free
it is time to forgive
time to choose to see

The blinding within
the blinding within
Universe eyes wide
I witness the other side

— *returning to the light*

Look at how powerful you are—
watch me
She says

And in the same breath
that she exalts Her salt particles
and churns to swallow you
the ocean cascades
into a costume of glass

Smoothing out Her hearts
swirling all of Her parts
each lung and limb
stretching into humility

I exhale the deepest moan
my womb didn't know it owned
I purge the air up through my throat
with eyes that tear-form two small
moats
my chest it pumps
the last energy I've got

My exhaust
folds me
collapsing at the knees

206

bowing down to the Mother
of all that has been seen

And it's in this moment
my warrioress-ness
remembers my potency
and how far I've trekked

For I have been storm
and am now graced peace
and I may be tumultuous
but I now shift more in ease

And I feel dark-deep in tidal waves
and in my own tides I've once drowned
but I've learned to swim among me
my own oceans I now surmount

— *learning from the ocean*

I will plant in your shadowy darkness
seeds that grow in the light
I will turn each of you
into flowers

— *vow to wounds*

Sun
you were loud and glory
thank you for your teachings
yet I fell to dried white coral
beneath you in sole

Darkness
you were mysterious and wise
thank you for your teachings
yet I starved on sharp ice
swallowed by you alone

Now
I've grown to shield with boundaries
to protect me while I bask
and I sparked the embers of my heart
to warm me while I rest

And still I bow down to you both
for shaping me from doubt
but I've relearned to rise to my feet—
it's the moon I dance with now

— falling in love with the moon

about the author

Olivia Morrissey is a poet, writer, healer and yogini. With a life lens of love, and never straying too far from the ocean, Olivia offers her time and energy reminding humans of the world of their truth: that they have always ever been love.

Olivia combines her linguistic passion with her certifications in Reiki healing, Yin and Vinyasa Yoga, and her experience in circle facilitation to hold space for empowered and sacred diving, release, and expression.

Fueled by the teachings of nature, her purpose is in deepening her understanding of interconnectedness, non-duality, and feminine and masculine energy. Her why is returning to the soft magnetism and sanctity of her own feminine energy and guiding humanity to remember the ancient wisdom of energetic balance as a collective.

Made in the USA
Middletown, DE
15 November 2020

24085987R00132